Original title:
The Quilt of Connection

Copyright © 2024 Swan Charm
All rights reserved.

Author: Kaido Väinamäe
ISBN HARDBACK: 978-9916-86-632-0
ISBN PAPERBACK: 978-9916-86-633-7
ISBN EBOOK: 978-9916-86-634-4

Harmonies in Fabric

Threads of color blend and sway,
Dancing softly, night and day.
Patterns whisper, stories call,
In every stitch, we weave it all.

Fabric spun from dreams and care,
Each piece crafted, love to share.
Textures mingle, hearts align,
In this tapestry, we shine.

Weaving Differences

Strands of varied hue unite,
Creating beauty, pure delight.
In the clash, we find our song,
Together, we are truly strong.

Threads may fray, but still they bind,
In our weave, we're intertwined.
Diversity, a vibrant thread,
Woven tales of dreams we've spread.

Quirks in the Weave

Odd patterns spark, a playful twist,
In the fabric, joy can't be missed.
Uneven stitches, stories told,
In hazy hues, our dreams unfold.

The quirkiness brings us near,
In every flaw, we find the cheer.
Textures dance, emotions sway,
In this quilt, we find our way.

Ties of Time

Threads of history gently fade,
Yet in the weave, they are displayed.
Moments captured, stitches tight,
In twilight's glow, they spark the night.

Eras blend in soft embrace,
Time erased, we've found our place.
With each knot, our stories grow,
In this fabric, memories flow.

Tied Together in Harmony

In the quiet of the night,
Our hearts beat as one,
Threads of dreams intertwine,
Under the watchful sun.

Voices blend in soft light,
Melodies sweet and clear,
Hand in hand, we take flight,
Cherished moments draw near.

Colors flourish and glow,
Each hue tells a tale,
Through laughter and through woe,
We set our own sail.

In the rhythms we sway,
Embracing the unknown,
Together we will play,
In harmony, we've grown.

With every step we share,
Life's dance paints the way,
United in our care,
We cherish every day.

Hand-stitched Whispers

In the fabric of our thoughts,
Secrets weave and spin,
Softly whispered, they are caught,
Where love and hope begin.

Each stitch a silent vow,
Crafted by hands so true,
In this moment, here and now,
I'll always cherish you.

Patterns formed with care,
Threads of joy and fears,
Life's tapestry we share,
Woven through the years.

Underneath the stars above,
We find our dreams align,
In the warmth of our love,
Every heart will shine.

And in whispers, we confide,
Stories yet to be,
With you always by my side,
Hand-stitched, we are free.

Confessions in Cloth

Beneath the weight of dreams,
Lies a tale untold,
In soft fabric, it gleams,
As truths begin to unfold.

Each thread a hidden fear,
Stitched with hope and grace,
In every whispered tear,
Love finds its rightful place.

The patterns speak in hues,
Dancing in the light,
Confessions in our views,
Illuminate the night.

With every seam we trace,
Our past begins to fade,
In the warmth of embrace,
New memories are made.

In cloth, we find release,
As stories intertwine,
Each moment brings us peace,
In fabric, love shall shine.

Symphonies in Squares

In corners bright, where colors blend,
Music dances, notes ascend.
Each sharp line, a clear refrain,
Harmonies in frames remain.

Patterns weave, a visual song,
In structures bold, we all belong.
A tapestry of sound and sight,
Composing joys in day and night.

Rhythms pulse through walls of light,
Echoes linger, soft and tight.
Art and life in union play,
Symphonies on display display.

Cascading shades, they spin and twirl,
In every square, the stories swirl.
Each angle sharp, they sing anew,
A joyful space where dreams break through.

Together we dance, in this place,
In every pattern, a warm embrace.
Symphonies in squares, they do call,
Inviting each heart, inspiring all.

Echoes of Empathy

In whispers soft, we share our truth,
Finding solace in the proof.
A quiet gaze, the bond we seek,
In gentle tones, our hearts will speak.

With hands extended, warmth we find,
A bridge between our hearts and mind.
In every act, compassion's grace,
An echo felt, in a safe space.

No words needed, we understand,
Connected by a steady hand.
Shared laughter, tears, and silent cries,
In these moments, love never lies.

From shadows cast, we rise as one,
Through storms endured, we see the sun.
With open hearts, we break the norm,
Together we find a brand new form.

Echoes linger in the air,
Building strength when we all share.
In unity, we find our way,
Empathy lights up the day.

Strands of Support

In tangled threads, we weave our plans,
Holding tight with gentle hands.
Through trials faced, we stand as one,
A fabric rich, together spun.

Each strand a story, strong and bold,
Connections made, worth more than gold.
In moments bright or shadows cast,
Together we can hold steadfast.

With every stitch, we mend the tears,
In laughter shared, we weave our cares.
A tapestry of hope and trust,
Intertwined, it's fair and just.

Woven closely through night and day,
In every challenge, we find a way.
The bonds we form, a steadfast guide,
In strands of love, we take our stride.

Support surrounds us, a sacred sphere,
In every heartbeat, we draw near.
In unity, we grow and rise,
With strands of support, we reach the skies.

Ties that Bind

In silent moments, we align,
The ties that bind through space and time.
With trust and care, we come to greet,
A circle strong beneath our feet.

Through laughter shared, and sorrows spent,
In every glance, a life well lent.
With open arms, we shelter grace,
A woven bond, our sacred place.

Through storms we brace, hand in hand,
With steadfast hearts, we understand.
In each encounter, threads unite,
A tapestry of shared delight.

The warmth we share, a glowing flame,
In this embrace, we lose the shame.
In joy and pain, we find our way,
Ties that bind never fray.

In every heartbeat, strong and clear,
The ties that bind, we hold so dear.
Together, forging paths of light,
In love and hope, we take our flight.

Mending the Fabric of Us

Threads of gold weave through the night,
Stitch by stitch, we hold on tight.
In every tear, a story glows,
Mending the fabric that life bestows.

Faded edges, we'll color anew,
With each heartbeat, our love is true.
Patterns dance in a rhythm sweet,
Together we rise, perfecting each beat.

Time may fray what we once knew,
Yet through the struggle, hope shines through.
Needles of care, weaving our dreams,
Unraveling joy, like sunlit beams.

In moments dark, we find the light,
A tapestry rich, woven in sight.
Each patch a memory, vibrant and bold,
Mending the fabric, a story retold.

Traces of Trust

In whispered winds, our vows arise,
Silent echoes beneath vast skies.
Each step we take, a promise shared,
Traces of trust, softly declared.

Time weaves threads both fragile and strong,
Bonding our hearts, where we belong.
In shadows long and silence deep,
Trust is the treasure we must keep.

Through storms that churn, and tides that sway,
We find our compass, guiding the way.
With every glance, our secrets unfold,
Traces of trust, a love untold.

In laughter shared and tears that fall,
We craft a shelter, strong through it all.
Hand in hand, we'll brave the dark,
Finding the light in every spark.

Patchwork Perspectives

Pieces stitched from dreams afar,
Each a glimpse, like a shining star.
In colors bright, our stories blend,
Patchwork perspectives, we transcend.

Tangled threads may cross and twine,
Creating beauty, by design.
Views from each heart, stitched side by side,
In the quilt of life, we take pride.

Voices echo, a chorus unique,
In harmony, our spirits speak.
Understanding blooms where patience grows,
Patchwork perspectives, our wisdom shows.

Through different lenses, we can see,
Together we shape our destiny.
In every patch, a tale reveals,
A tapestry rich, time heals.

An Array of Affection

In gentle waves, our love's embrace,
An array of affection, soft and grace.
With every touch, a spark ignites,
Filling our days with radiant lights.

Like petals falling from a bloom,
Love flourishes, dispels the gloom.
In quiet moments, our hearts align,
An array of affection, so divine.

Through laughter shared and whispered dreams,
Life's journey flows in radiant streams.
In every glance, warmth and delight,
An array of affection, pure and bright.

Colors blend in the softest way,
Painting love's story day by day.
Hand in hand, our spirits soar,
An array of affection, forevermore.

Fabric of Familiarity

In the quiet of the room, we pause,
Memories linger like soft whispers.
Time threads through our laughter's seams,
Binding us close in woven dreams.

With every glance, a story shared,
The fabric of life, carefully bared.
Patterns of joy dance in the air,
Threads of love, a bond so rare.

Through trials faced and joys embraced,
In every heart, a common place.
Familiar voices hum a tune,
Calming the wildness of the moon.

As moments fade and seasons shift,
We hold the warmth, a precious gift.
In every stitch, a tale we weave,
The fabric of familiarity we believe.

Together we stand, hand in hand,
In this tapestry finely planned.
With every heartbeat, we are sewn,
In the depths of love, we have grown.

Tapestry of Shared Dreams

In the quiet night, our dreams align,
Stitched together, your heart and mine.
Colors of hope blend in the sky,
Patterned moments where wishes fly.

Through the loom of time, we create,
A tapestry of trust, strong as fate.
Every thread tells a story bright,
Bringing us closer, shedding light.

In laughter's echo, we find our way,
Guided by stars that brightly stay.
With every challenge, our threads unite,
Weaving strength through the darkest night.

A canvas vast, where visions roam,
In shared dreams, we build our home.
With every heartbeat, tales are spun,
Joining our spirits, two into one.

As dawn approaches, colors unfold,
A tapestry rich with stories told.
In the embrace of dawn's warm beam,
We dance together, in shared dreams.

Interwoven Lives

In the loom of life, our paths entwine,
With every heartbeat, your hand in mine.
Threads of kindness, soft and true,
We weave through days, me and you.

With laughter echoing in the air,
Interwoven lives we gently share.
In sorrow's shadow, we find the light,
Binding our hearts, a beautiful sight.

Through every challenge, we stand tall,
No thread too frayed can make us fall.
In the fabric of moments, we embrace,
Cherishing every line on our face.

Seasons fade, but love remains,
In every stitch, our joy sustains.
Together we journey, side by side,
In the weave of life, we abide.

As the tapestry grows, stories gleam,
Reflecting the beauty of our shared dreams.
Through the ebb and flow, our spirits thrive,
In the interwoven lives, we come alive.

Embracing the Common Thread

In the tapestry of every day,
Threads of life find their own way.
Colors blend, as feelings meld,
Embracing moments, stories held.

Our hearts speak in familiar tones,
In the laughter, there are no bones.
Caring glances, warm and bright,
Illuminating the darkest night.

Every challenge faced becomes a spark,
In the embrace, we leave a mark.
Navigating paths, hand in hand,
In the common thread, we understand.

With woven love, we face our fears,
Through shared dreams and joyful tears.
In every fiber, the truth unfolds,
The warmth of connection, a story told.

As we gather round, old and new,
The common thread binds me to you.
In the tapestry, rich and vast,
We weave our futures, holding the past.

Coalescing Colors

In the canvas of the sky,
Brushes dip in vibrant hues,
Strokes of joy and whispers soft,
Creating worlds we choose.

Reds and blues in a dance,
Twirl and spin with grace,
Nature's palette sings aloud,
In this sacred space.

Golden suns meet emerald trees,
Shadows play with fleeting light,
Every shade a story told,
In the warmth of night.

Textures blend, horizons bend,
In twilight's gentle touch,
Colors merge in symphony,
A world, oh, it's so much.

Together in a splendid word,
The beauty draws us near,
Coalescing in soft whispers,
Colors bright, sincere.

Fabricated Futures

Blueprints lay on dusty shelves,
Dreams etched in clarity,
Visions dance in silver threads,
Of what's meant to be.

Skyscrapers built with hopes alive,
Each floor, a tale profound,
Windows glinting with the past,
A future waiting found.

Gears are turning, hearts are bold,
In the forge of our design,
Crafting lives from scattered sparks,
Turning dust into shine.

Paths entwine like woven ropes,
Together, we shall stand,
Fabricated futures bright,
With an open hand.

A tapestry of hands and dreams,
Unity, our guiding star,
Together, we create the world,
No matter where we are.

Warmth Woven Among Us

Threads of laughter, echoes near,
Stitched through every day,
With kindness woven in each heart,
In a tender way.

Moments shared, a gentle touch,
Wraps the chill away,
In the fabric of our lives,
Love is here to stay.

Soft embraces gathered close,
Holding fears at bay,
A quilt of souls, together strong,
In this warm array.

Every smile, a thread of light,
Binds us as we soar,
Woven deep in friendship's guise,
Always wanting more.

Together in this woven dance,
No colder night can find,
Warmth thrives among the seams,
Hearts and hopes aligned.

Embraces in Every Fold

Beneath the layers, history hides,
Wisdom wrapped in time,
Each fold holds tender secrets,
In rhythm and in rhyme.

A gentle breath, a whispered word,
In the fabric's embrace,
Cocooned within soft stories,
Time leaves not a trace.

In every crease, a memory blooms,
Love stitched in every seam,
A tapestry of hope and tears,
Together in a dream.

Each twist and turn of life we face,
Is cradled close and tight,
For in these folds, we find our strength,
Emerging from the night.

Embraces deep, within each fold,
Life's intricate design,
Together we unveil our souls,
A journey smooth and fine.

Colors of Companionship

In every hue, our laughter blooms,
A tapestry of joy in rooms.
Through sunny days and stormy weather,
We paint our hearts, forever together.

The blues of peace in quiet nights,
Golden moments filled with lights.
The greens of growth, the reds of cheer,
In every shade, I hold you near.

In vibrant scenes, our friendship thrives,
Each stroke of love, it deepens lives.
We blend our stories, bright and bold,
A masterpiece in every fold.

With brushes dipped in dreams untold,
We sketch our future, brave and gold.
In every corner, warmth does dwell,
In colors shared, we weave our spell.

Linked by Legacy

In shadows cast by years we've grown,
Our roots entwined, together sown.
With every story passed along,
A bond is forged, a timeless song.

Through whispered tales of those before,
We build a bridge, we learn, explore.
In echoes of our family's pride,
A legacy that won't subside.

Each memory, a precious thread,
In fabric rich, our hearts are spread.
Through trials faced and triumphs earned,
The fire of kinship brightly burned.

United strong, we rise as one,
A tapestry beneath the sun.
In every stitch, our lives entwined,
Linked by legacy, love defined.

Stitching Shared Memories

In every stitch, a moment we place,
We sew our laughter, our joys we trace.
With hands together, we create art,
Stitched with memories, sewn from the heart.

The fabric tells of days gone by,
Of secrets whispered and dreams that fly.
Each patch recalls the smiles we shared,
In every thread, our hearts laid bare.

With vibrant colors, our stories blend,
A quilt of love that knows no end.
We piece together what life unfolds,
In woven tales, our hearts consoled.

Through joys and sorrows, we carry on,
In every square, a tale is drawn.
Together we craft this beautiful seam,
Our journey stitched, a shared dream.

Fabricated Fables

In whispered tales by candlelight,
Fabricated fables take their flight.
With every word, a world we weave,
In stories spun, we dare believe.

From ancient myths to dreams anew,
In timeless bonds, our hearts are true.
We share the tales of brave and bold,
In every line, the magic told.

In woven stories, we find our place,
Each fable crafted with gentle grace.
Through laughter, tears, the fabric bends,
In every chapter, our spirit mends.

With threads of wonder, we spin our fate,
In dreams and hopes, we navigate.
In every fable, a lesson learned,
In hearts entwined, the flame still burned.

Patterns of Belonging

In the dance of shadows, we find our place,
Woven in laughter, our spirits embrace.
Threads of connection, both tangled and clear,
Echoes of stories we hold very dear.

On the canvas of life, we paint with our hands,
Brushstrokes of memories, where love understands.
Colors of friendship in bright, vivid hues,
Together we navigate paths we choose.

Through the storms of doubt, we steady our sails,
Bound by the whispers, where trust never fails.
In the moments of silence, our hearts speak loud,
Patterns of belonging, we wear like a shroud.

With every heartbeat, a rhythm unfolds,
Stories of triumph and courage retold.
In a world of chaos, we find our song,
United in purpose, where we all belong.

In the tapestry woven, each thread has a tale,
Intertwined destinies like echoes in pale.
Together we'll flourish, forever we'll stand,
In patterns of belonging, hand in hand.

Interlaced Journeys

Two paths converging under the stars,
Traveling onward, leaving behind scars.
Winding in circles, we seek and we find,
Journeys interlaced, our fates intertwined.

With every new step, a story we share,
Moments wrapped gently, with love and with care.
The laughter of children, the wisdom of age,
In the book of our lives, we turn every page.

Mountains are crossed, and oceans we brave,
Together as one, we learn how to save.
Casting our dreams into skies far and wide,
In interlaced journeys, we ebb and we tide.

Through valleys of doubt and peaks of delight,
Hand in hand moving, we ignite the night.
Stories of courage, we cherish and hold,
Creating a legacy, vibrant and bold.

In the rhythm of travel, we dance to our fate,
Mapping out moments, a fellowship great.
In the highlight of life, let's savor each turn,
In interlaced journeys, together we learn.

Tapestry of Hearts

Threads of affection, we weave day by day,
Together we build, come what may.
Colors of passion, in every embrace,
Stitching our dreams in a vibrant space.

With laughter and tears, our fabric grows strong,
A tapestry woven where all can belong.
Silken connections that never shall fray,
In the warmth of our hearts, love finds its way.

Knots of remembrance, we tie in our past,
Echoes of friendships, forever to last.
Each moment a pattern, a bond that we share,
In this tapestry of hearts, we'll always care.

Through storms we have weathered, through trials we've
faced,
The beauty of unity cannot be replaced.
Wrap us in kindness, and let colors blend,
In this tapestry of hearts, love is our thread.

As seasons keep changing, our fibers stay true,
Interwoven destinies, me and you.
In every heartbeat, our stories impart,
A living, breathing tapestry of hearts.

Connective Fabrications

In the fabric of life, let's stitch every dream,
Weaving together, a collective scheme.
Patterns emerging, unique yet aligned,
Connective fabrications, with hearts intertwined.

From whispers of kindness and laughter so bright,
We build a foundation, our guiding light.
Every shared moment a thread in our cloth,
Connecting us gently, from east into north.

Through trials and triumphs, our tapestry grows,
Stitched with resilience, where love overflows.
In the glow of our stories, together we stand,
Crafted through trials, forever we'll band.

Embroidered with courage, each line tells of grace,
In this intricate weaving, we find our place.
Every twist, every turn, a fabric well spun,
In connective fabrications, we are each one.

Linked by our dreams, in colors we share,
This grand design makes us wonderfully rare.
In the warmth of connection, we flourish and grow,
In connective fabrications, love will always flow.

Arc of Interwoven Stories

In the fabric of time, we weave,
Tales hidden in patterns we believe.
Each thread a whisper, a moment untold,
Binding the past with the future we hold.

Stitch by stitch, we craft our fate,
Entangled in love, loss, and debate.
A tapestry bright with colors so bold,
Stories of silver, of bronze, and of gold.

Underneath laughter, tears deeply flow,
In the shadows of light, our truths start to grow.
Every wrinkle a memory, every fold a heart,
In this arc of stories, we each play our part.

As the loom spins tales of heart's delight,
Threads of the day dance into the night.
In every stitch lies a hope, a dream,
Woven together, we are more than we seem.

Embroidered with hope, fears left behind,
An intricate journey of heart and mind.
Through the arcs we wander, through stories we roam,
In this fabric of life, together we're home.

Stitched Together

Every fragment tells a tale,
Of struggles faced and dreams set sail.
With needle in hand, we mend and repair,
Stitched together with love and with care.

Each patch a symbol of journeys taken,
Of bonds that were formed, and hearts that awaken.
In the quilt of our lives, colors start to blend,
Whispers that echo, where memories transcend.

Layers upon layers, we carefully place,
A tapestry woven of every embrace.
In the seams of our laughter, tears start to flow,
Stitched together in harmony, we grow.

As days unfold in patterns designed,
The stitches we share forever aligned.
Bound by the threads of a shared history,
Together we are, as we strive to be free.

A beautiful chaos, a dance of the heart,
From many pieces, we craft our own art.
In this patchwork, we find strength to weather,
Hand in hand, forever stitched together.

The Harmony of Threads

In each fiber lies a secret tune,
A melody rising with the light of the moon.
Threads intertwine with graceful ease,
Creating a dance that carries the breeze.

With whispers of color, they softly sing,
Of unity found in the joy they bring.
As patterns emerge from chaos and strife,
In the harmony of threads, we weave our life.

A tapestry painted with strokes of delight,
Each line a journey that reaches new height.
In the rhythm of weaving, hearts open wide,
Together in harmony, we take each stride.

Fading echoes of moments we share,
In the fabric of existence, love fills the air.
Stitching our stories, we grow ever bold,
In the harmony of threads, futures unfold.

As the loom spins tales of love's gentle song,
In this woven embrace, we all belong.
Each thread a note in this sacred choir,
Together we rise, ascending higher.

Unseen Patterns

Beneath the surface, mysteries spin,
In the depths of our hearts, new journeys begin.
Threads intertwine in a dance of creation,
Unseen patterns weave our foundation.

Invisible ties pull us ever near,
Crafting connections we hold so dear.
In the quiet spaces where shadows may play,
The threads of our stories find light in the gray.

As we search for meaning in places unknown,
Each stitch holds a truth, even when alone.
In the tapestry's folds, life's secrets reside,
Unseen patterns guide us, our faithful guide.

Canvas of life, painted with grace,
In the quiet corners, we each find our place.
Through winding paths, our fates intertwine,
In the unseen patterns, your heart meets mine.

As we navigate the threads of our fate,
In this woven wonder, we find what we create.
Together we stand, though sometimes apart,
Embracing the unseen with an open heart.

The Patchwork of Us

We stitch our stories, hand in hand,
With every moment, we understand.
Tales woven tight in laughter's embrace,
Creating a tapestry time can't erase.

Each patch a memory, both bright and dim,
The colors of courage, we wear on a whim.
In threads of compassion, we find our way,
Through storms and sunshine, come what may.

When shadows dance, we hold on strong,
In the patchwork of us, where we belong.
Each fragment a whisper, a promise we've made,
In the quilt of our lives, love won't ever fade.

Together we stand, through thick and thin,
With hearts like anchors, we always win.
In the fabric of time, our essence we weave,
With every thread spun, we truly believe.

Forever entwined, we aim for the skies,
In the patchwork of us, forever we rise.

Interwoven Dreams

In moonlit nights, our dreams take flight,
Through starlit paths, we chase the light.
Each vision a promise, a wish to behold,
In the fabric of hope, our stories unfold.

With threads of ambition, we stitch our fate,
Together we rise, never too late.
A dance of ideas, so free and wild,
In this realm of dreams, both tender and wild.

We craft our futures, with shadows and light,
In the heart of the night, we take our flight.
With courage as our compass, we soar on high,
In the tapestry of dreams, together we fly.

Each plan a pattern, uniquely designed,
In the weave of our hopes, forever entwined.
With laughter as ink, we pen our tale,
Interwoven dreams, we will never fail.

Through the ebb and flow, we trust our way,
In this canvas of life, come what may.
With every heartbeat, our visions gleam,
In the tapestry of us, we weave our dream.

Bonds Beneath the Surface

Beneath the laughter, secrets lie,
A current of love that won't say goodbye.
In silent glances, a language we speak,
A bond so deep, yet never feels weak.

Through storms and struggles, we stand firm,
In the depths of our hearts, we find our term.
Each quiet moment, a treasure we share,
In the bonds we nurture, there's always care.

Like roots intertwined, we grow so strong,
In the garden of trust, we both belong.
Underneath the surface, our spirits dance,
In the rhythm of life, we take a chance.

When words escape, we still understand,
With a touch, a gesture, a gentle hand.
In the silence between, love finds its way,
In the bonds beneath, we'll always stay.

Together we thrive, through thick and thin,
In the depths of together, we always win.
With every heartbeat, our stories entwine,
In the bonds beneath, our souls align.

Knots of Compassion

In the fabric of kindness, we tie our knots,
Each gesture a thread, connecting the spots.
With love as the anchor, we hold it tight,
In the knots of compassion, we shine so bright.

Through trials we weave, a tapestry strong,
In moments of weakness, we still belong.
With every embrace, we soften the pain,
In the knots of compassion, love will remain.

With hands that uplift, we gather like rain,
In the circle of hope, we lighten the strain.
Each knot a reminder of what we can be,
In the bonds we create, we truly are free.

Through struggle and strife, we stand side by side,
With hearts open wide, compassion our guide.
Together we journey, with grace we align,
In the knots of compassion, our futures entwine.

In quiet moments, our spirits connect,
In every small act, we truly reflect.
Through love's gentle hands, we thrive, we grow,
In the knots of compassion, our essence will flow.

Harmony in Patchwork

Threads of color, woven tight,
Stories whispered in the night,
Each stitch a bond, a tale to share,
A tapestry of love and care.

In patterns bright, emotions flow,
Hearts united, we gently sow,
A quilt of dreams, both old and new,
Together we create the view.

Textures mingle, soft and grand,
In warm embrace, we take a stand,
Harmony found in every seam,
A patchwork life, a shared dream.

Through every fray, we find our song,
In unity, we all belong,
A blend of joy, we treasure true,
In every square, I see our hue.

So let us weave with gentle hands,
Through life's journey, as time expands,
Together we rise, forever bold,
In harmony, our hearts unfold.

Mosaic of Memories

Fragments scattered on the floor,
Each piece holds a life before,
Golden laughter, shadows cast,
In this mosaic, moments last.

A child's smile, bright and loud,
In the colors, we feel proud,
Echoes of a distant past,
In every shard, a love amassed.

Soft whispers, secrets shared,
In the tiles, a heart laid bare,
Memories dance, a vibrant hue,
A patchwork of me and you.

Brighter days, some painted blue,
In this art, our journeys grew,
An album of our stories told,
In every piece, our lives unfold.

Together we create this space,
With every memory we embrace,
A living art, forever shines,
In mosaic, true love aligns.

Tufts of Trust

In the garden, trust does grow,
Soft tufts of green in a row,
Rooted deep in soil so rich,
A bond that time will not unitch.

Gentle whispers on the breeze,
Promises as sweet as trees,
Together we thrive, hand in hand,
In this sacred, loving land.

With every moment, seeds are sown,
In trust, we find our way back home,
A fortress built on faith and truth,
In tufts of trust, eternal youth.

Sunrise breaks, our hearts awake,
In every choice, the paths we make,
A vibrant tapestry of care,
In strength of trust, we all can share.

So let us nurture, let us feed,
The tufts of trust, our greatest need,
In quiet moments, side by side,
In the garden, love won't hide.

Warmth in a Fabricated World

Amidst the cold, a fire glows,
In every heart, a kindness shows,
In fabricated walls we stand,
Together, woven hand in hand.

With every smile, the warmth ignites,
In fleeting days and starry nights,
We build a haven, safe and true,
In the warmth, I find my cue.

Gentle gestures, soft and bright,
In laughter shared, we find the light,
A beacon in the darkest air,
In this great world, love's everywhere.

With each embrace, we break the mold,
Creating warmth within the fold,
Fabricated ties, yet so real,
In love's embrace, our hearts can heal.

So let us share this glowing flame,
In a world that seeks to tame,
Together we'll shine, forever bold,
In the warmth, our stories told.

Frayed Edges of Love

In whispers soft, love's fabric frays,
The colors blend in tender ways.
Each stitch a promise, worn with care,
Yet still we find the threads to share.

Faded edges tell our tale,
Through storm and sun, we will not pale.
In shadows cast, our hearts entwine,
Frayed edges shine with love divine.

With every tear, new stitches made,
Through trials faced, our bond won't fade.
The tapestry of us grows bold,
In frayed edges, stories told.

So let us weave with hands that know,
The beauty found in love's soft glow.
For every thread that wears away,
Brings us closer, day by day.

Through every challenge, still we stand,
With open hearts and steady hands.
In frayed edges, love's beauty lies,
A masterpiece beneath the skies.

Threads that Tell

Threads that weave through time and space,
Each moment shared, a silken trace.
With vibrant hues, our stories blend,
In tangled knots that never end.

From laughter's echo to silent tears,
Each thread a map of all our years.
In patterns bold and gentle lines,
Our hearts connect where love defines.

The distant past and future's call,
In every stitch, we rise, we fall.
These threads of life, so deftly spun,
Together, we have just begun.

A tapestry of dreams and hopes,
With every turn, our spirit copes.
Threads that tell of joy and strife,
Embroidering the tale of life.

So take my hand, let's weave anew,
In threads of gold and azure blue.
For every story that we share,
Is stitched in love, beyond compare.

Bonded by the Needle

With needle sharp and thread so fine,
We stitch our lives through moments divine.
Each tiny puncture shows the pain,
Yet holds the joy, like sun after rain.

In whispered dreams, we pull it tight,
A bond that glimmers in the night.
Sewn with hope and gentle grace,
We find our strength in this embrace.

Each knot a promise, firm and true,
In every color, shades of you.
Together weaving, hand in hand,
A tapestry both bright and grand.

Through frayed edges and tangled seams,
We build our world from fragile dreams.
Bound by love, through thick and thin,
With every stitch, our lives begin.

So let the needle dance and glide,
As we hold fast, with hearts open wide.
For in each stitch, a love unfurls,
Bonded tightly in this swirling world.

Stitched Hearts

In quiet moments, hearts entwine,
With every stitch, our souls align.
Threads of passion, joy, and pain,
Stitched together in love's softer reign.

From fragments lost to wholeness gained,
Through laughter shared and tears unchained.
We sew our dreams with colors bright,
Stitched hearts glowing in the night.

Each loop a promise, each pull a sigh,
In this craft where two can lie.
Together we create and mend,
In every twist, our lives extend.

So take this quilt, so warm and wide,
With stitched hearts beating side by side.
In every square a memory spun,
Together we are always one.

As time goes on, we'll still create,
New patterns in love's canvas great.
With every fiber, we'll remain,
Stitched hearts dancing through joy and pain.

Sewn Together by Stories

In a quilt of tales we weave,
Embroidered dreams that we believe.
Each stitch a laugh, each tear a sigh,
Bound by secrets, you and I.

Threads of color, bright and bold,
Stitched in warmth, in love retold.
We gather moments, soft and sweet,
Each shared story makes us complete.

From whispered nights to sunny days,
In every pattern, our hearts play.
Together in this tapestry,
We find our truth in unity.

Every square a memory, dear,
In the fabric, joy and fear.
Together stitched, we shall remain,
In the quilt of life, our shared pain.

So let our stories intertwine,
A patchwork life, so divine.
Hand in hand, we boldly tread,
Sewn together until we're dead.

Tangles of Time

Time weaves threads both thin and thick,
In patterns strange, it plays its trick.
Moments slip like grains of sand,
Tangled pathways, unplanned.

Memories dance in shades of grey,
Fleeting whispers, here to stay.
In every tick, a story told,
In silence warm, the past unfolds.

Through tangled knots, we seek the light,
Finding comfort in the night.
Paths may cross, then drift away,
Yet echoes of love always stay.

Seasons change with gentle grace,
In every line, a timeless trace.
Connections wane and then ignite,
In tangled threads, all feels right.

So here we stand, amidst the weave,
In tangled time, we learn to believe.
Each moment cherished, every rhyme,
A melody lost in tangled time.

Fragments of Friendship

In pieces bright, our friendship glows,
Each fragment holds what kindness sows.
Scattered shards of laughter clear,
In every break, a bond draws near.

We share our hearts in quiet ways,
As sunlight warms the cloudy days.
In mirrored smiles, the truth we find,
Fragments join, our souls aligned.

Through trials faced, through bitter storms,
We find our strength in quirky forms.
A puzzle made of love and care,
In every piece, our hearts laid bare.

Though time may stretch, and paths may part,
In every beat, you hold my heart.
Together woven, never alone,
In fragments deep, our love has grown.

So raise a glass to memories sweet,
To fragments that make us feel complete.
In every piece, a story shared,
In friendship's warmth, we're always spared.

Needle and Narrative

With needle poised, the tales begin,
A quiet hum, a gentle spin.
Each thread brings silence to the scream,
In every stitch, we weave a dream.

Narratives flow like rivers wide,
In fabric soft, our truths reside.
A tapestry of hopes and fears,
Each knot a bridge that binds our years.

Stories loop and intertwine,
Bringing light to every line.
With every pull, the tale unfolds,
In needle's dance, new worlds are told.

So let us sew with fervent care,
Each thread a vow, a whispered prayer.
As long as voices share their song,
In needle's art, we all belong.

In the fabric of life's embrace,
We find our stories, we find our place.
Together stitched, forever strong,
A narrative rich, we all belong.

Stitches of Solitude

In quiet corners, shadows play,
A single thread, it leads away.
The fabric of thoughts, finely spun,
In solitude's grasp, I come undone.

The needle pricks, it hurts to know,
Each stitch a whisper, soft and slow.
Alone I dwell, in threads of time,
A tapestry made, from silent rhyme.

Through empty nights, the fabric weaves,
In solitude, the heart believes.
Patterns of longing, shadows of light,
A quilt of memories, wrapped so tight.

Each stitch a story, woven deep,
In dreams of solace, softly sleep.
With every tug, the heart will mend,
As solitude teaches, we learn to bend.

Yet in the seams, a strength is found,
In silence, beauty does abound.
Through threads of life, by hand designed,
The stitches bind, our souls aligned.

Threads of Togetherness

In colors bright, two hearts entwine,
Together weaving, design divine.
With laughter's thread and dreams so bold,
A tapestry of love unfolds.

Through sunlit days and starry nights,
We stitch our stories, in shared delights.
Each gentle tug, a bond we share,
In every thread, a promise there.

From different paths, we come to one,
With every loop, our fears undone.
In vibrant hues, our dreams align,
Together crafting, a life so fine.

The warmth of hands, a touch so near,
In woven bonds, we have no fear.
Threads of joy, in harmony,
Together stitched, our destiny.

With every stitch, our hearts take flight,
In threads of love, we find our light.
Through time and space, our bond will grow,
In the tapestry of life, we glow.

Woven Whispers

In the twilight hour, whispers creep,
Between the stitches, secrets keep.
A gentle brush, of fabric soft,
In woven words, our spirits loft.

With every seam, a tale is spun,
Of cherished moments, two become one.
The threads we share, in twilight's hue,
Woven whispers, a bond so true.

The fabric sings, with every tear,
In woven forms, our hearts lay bare.
In quiet corners, stories tease,
With every breath, the heart finds ease.

Amidst the stitches, laughter plays,
A tapestry of our brighter days.
The threads of life, so finely kissed,
In woven whispers, we coexist.

From whispered dreams to laughter's call,
In every weave, we rise, we fall.
Together intertwined, we sway,
In woven whispers, come what may.

Fabric of Bonds

In every thread, a tale is spun,
A fabric woven, two become one.
With colored strands, we weave our fate,
In bonds of love, we celebrate.

From distant shores, our paths unite,
Through every challenge, we find our light.
In every twist and every turn,
The fabric speaks, together we learn.

With hands entwined, we stitch our dreams,
In vibrant hues, our laughter gleams.
From shared moments, a quilt is sewn,
In the fabric of bonds, we have grown.

The warmth of hearts, in every seam,
Through threads of hope, we chase our dream.
With every knot, our love's embrace,
In the fabric of bonds, we find our place.

So let us weave, with care and grace,
Each thread a memory, time cannot erase.
In the tapestry of life, we stand,
United forever, hand in hand.

Unity in Every Stitch

In every thread, a bond is made,
We come together, unafraid.
Stronger hands and hearts align,
In this fabric, we define.

Through colors bright, a vision shared,
With every loop, we have declared.
Differences fade, together we rise,
In unity, we find the prize.

A tapestry of dreams unfolds,
Stories woven, blessings told.
From every stitch, a tale is spun,
In harmony, we are all one.

With patience, love, and care we sew,
Threads of hope in every flow.
Together we build, together we stand,
In this quilt, a loving hand.

So here's our pledge, forever strong,
In every seam, where we belong.
Unity shines in every stitch,
Crafted with love, no heart will glitch.

Seamless Encounters

Paths intertwine like threads in a loom,
A dance of souls, dispelling gloom.
In fleeting glances, a spark ignites,
Bridging the gaps, creating lights.

Every meeting, a stitch in time,
Connections form in rhythm and rhyme.
A shared laugh, a knowing glance,
In seamless moments, hearts enhance.

Blends of cultures, colors so bright,
Together we shine, banishing night.
With open hearts, we greet the day,
In each encounter, we find our way.

Embrace the bonds, let love be known,
In diverse threads, a friendship grown.
Seamless encounters weave the tale,
With every note, our voices sail.

Counted not by time, but by the heart,
In every ending, a fresh new start.
Through seamless ties, we find our place,
In togetherness, we leave a trace.

The Weave of Life

Under the sun, the fibers twist,
Joining hands in an endless mist.
Threads of sorrow, threads of cheer,
In the weave of life, we persevere.

Every moment, a strand is spun,
Ties that bind us, never undone.
Through trials faced and joys embraced,
In this tapestry, love is laced.

Patterns shift, yet we remain,
Learning strength through loss and gain.
Color and texture, rich and bold,
The weave of life, a story told.

With gentle hands, we mend the seams,
Crafting futures from our dreams.
In laughter bright or shadows cast,
The weave of life, forever vast.

So let us celebrate this thread,
For every moment, a life well led.
In unity and purpose, we thrive,
Together we make the weave alive.

Patches of Kinship

In patches stitched from memories fair,
We find our kinship, a bond so rare.
Every square tells a story true,
In vibrant hues, our love breaks through.

From different lands, we come to share,
In every patch, we show we care.
Stitched with laughter, sewn with tears,
In kinship, we conquer fears.

Threads of family, old and new,
In every seam, a love that grew.
United colors, strong and bright,
In patches of kinship, we find our light.

With every quilt, a tale reveals,
Of joy and heartache, love that heals.
Together we make this fabric whole,
In warmth and kindness, we console.

So cherish the patches that form our way,
In every thread, in night and day.
For kinship forged in love's embrace,
Makes this world a warmer place.

Borders of Belonging

In the soft glow of twilight,
We gather under stars that shine.
Whispers of home fill the air,
Hearts intertwined, yours and mine.

Familiar faces all around,
Binding threads of shared delight.
Each smile a promise bestowed,
In this warmth, we find our light.

Walls may rise and rivers flow,
Yet love transcends every space.
In every laugh, in every tear,
We find our way, our rightful place.

Every journey leaves a trace,
Stories echo, tales unfold.
Our roots run deep in this embrace,
Through every storm, together, bold.

So here we stand, hand in hand,
Crafting dreams where hope belongs.
In the hearts of those who care,
We weave the world, a tapestry of songs.

Weaves of Wisdom

In quiet corners of the mind,
Threads of thoughts begin to blend.
Wisdom whispered through the years,
Beneath each lesson, a friend.

The fabric of life is rich and deep,
Patterns change, but still remain.
Each thread a moment, tough or sweet,
In the weave, joy dances with pain.

Listen close to nature's call,
Every rustle, every sound.
In the silence lies the truth,
Where deeper wisdom can be found.

With every choice, we stitch anew,
Colors bright against the gray.
Life's a tapestry in motion,
Woven moments in bold display.

So let us ponder, let us learn,
Seek the light in every scar.
For in the weaves of wisdom, dear,
We find our way, no matter how far.

Layers of Affection

Beneath the surface, warmth resides,
Soft whispers blend with gentle sighs.
Each layer wraps around the heart,
A quilt of love that never dies.

Moments shared like autumn leaves,
Crimson and gold in vibrant cheer.
Every glance a silent vow,
In the storm, we are drawn near.

Fingers trace the paths we walk,
Carving memories in the air.
In every hug, a promise kept,
A sanctuary, safe and rare.

Love unfolds like petals bright,
Soft and fragrant, full of grace.
In the depths of shared laughter,
We find our own, a sacred space.

So cherish every tender note,
For these layers bind us whole.
In the warmth of affection's glow,
We find our way, we find our soul.

Interlacing Journeys

Two paths crossing in the dusk,
Fates entwined like vines that grow.
Each step forward, hearts in sync,
In the dance of life, we flow.

Footprints linger on the sand,
Stories etched in time's embrace.
With every turn, new worlds await,
Exploring depths and hidden space.

Through valleys low and mountains high,
We share our fears, our dreams in sight.
Together, we brave the vast unknown,
Guided by the moon's soft light.

Each journey teaches, every mile,
A tapestry of hopes and fears.
Together we rise, together we fall,
In laughter, love, and silent tears.

So let us wander, hand in hand,
With open hearts, we choose to roam.
In interlacing journeys, dear,
We find our strength, we find our home.

Ties That Bind

In shadows where whispers seem to play,
We find our paths, not far away.
Through laughter, tears, moments we share,
A bond unbroken, forever rare.

The thread of trust we weave with care,
In silence, our hearts laid bare.
Through storms we stand, side by side,
Love's gentle anchor is our guide.

Embracing flaws, we rise above,
In every challenge, we're wrapped in love.
Through every trial, hand in hand,
Together we walk, together we stand.

With every glance, a story told,
In warmth of friendship, hearts unfold.
These ties that bind, they never fray,
In the dance of life, we find our way.

As years go by, our roots run deep,
In the garden of memories, we lovingly keep.
Through time and change, we will remain,
In the tapestry of life, there's joy in pain.

Textures of Affinity

In the fabric of life, threads intertwine,
Colors of friendship, surely divine.
Patterns emerging, a vibrant spark,
In the daylight's warmth, dispelling the dark.

Each texture a story, a unique thread,
Of laughter and struggle, of words unsaid.
With every layer, a bond we feel,
In the embrace of softness, we heal.

The rhythm of hearts as they beat in tune,
Under the gaze of the silver moon.
In the depths of silence, understanding flows,
A masterpiece crafted, where love only grows.

Weaving dreams with delicate care,
In the garden of trust, blossoms rare.
Every echo a testament to time,
In the artistry of life, we rhyme.

Textures of affinity, rich and profound,
In the harmony of souls, we are found.
Tangled yet free in this beautiful dance,
Embracing the journey, seizing the chance.

Embracing Variations

In life's vast canvas, colors collide,
Each hue a reflection of what we hide.
With open hearts, we celebrate,
The beauty in differences, we cultivate.

Every voice adds harmony to our song,
In a world so vast, where we belong.
Through laughter, tears, each moment shared,
In our unique ways, we are bared.

The tapestry woven, intricate and bright,
Each thread a story that takes its flight.
In the dance of variations, we find grace,
In the unity of chaos, we embrace.

Through the lens of love, we see anew,
The myriad colors of me and you.
In every heartbeat, a rhythm divine,
In this symphony of life, we align.

Embracing variations, we grow tall,
In the garden of differences, we stand small.
With open arms and open minds,
In every soul, a treasure finds.

In Harmony's Embrace

In the quiet of night, stars softly gleam,
A perfect reflection of every dream.
As melodies whisper through the trees,
In harmony's embrace, hearts find ease.

With the rhythm of waves crashing ashore,
Echoing love that opens each door.
In the stillness, a song unfolds,
Of connections cherished, and stories told.

Every heartbeat sings a tune so sweet,
In the dance of the world, we find our beat.
Side by side, as life weaves its art,
In unity's grace, we'll never part.

In laughter and light, we intertwine,
In the richness of love, our spirits align.
Through seasons that change, our bond will grow,
In harmony's embrace, we'll forever glow.

Through trials faced and joys we share,
In the warmth of friendship, we breathe our air.
In the symphony of life, we find our place,
In harmony's embrace, love's endless grace.

Threads of Togetherness

In the garden of our dreams,
Colorful threads intertwine,
We share our hopes and schemes,
In each other's hearts, we shine.

With laughter woven tight,
We create a tapestry bright,
Through storms, our bond stands right,
Together, we face the night.

Each moment, a stitch we take,
In a quilt of love we make,
Every joy, every ache,
Unraveled, but never to break.

As seasons come and go,
Our threads will always flow,
In unity, we grow,
Together, we steal the show.

With every thread we spin,
A journey we begin,
Love's fabric, deep within,
Together, we gladly win.

Weaving Whispers of the Heart

In silence, whispers flow,
Words unspoken, soft and low,
Threads of feeling start to show,
Heartstrings pulled as feelings grow.

In the loom of night we share,
Secrets flutter through the air,
With gentle whispers, we declare,
A tapestry of love and care.

Each silver thread has its place,
Woven with warmth, time can't erase,
In quiet moments, find the grace,
Love's reflection in our embrace.

As dawn breaks, dreams take flight,
We continue our dance of light,
In whispers, we ignite the night,
Two souls bound, a beautiful sight.

Forever entwined in this art,
Threads of whispers, never apart,
Together we craft from the start,
The woven essence of the heart.

Stitches of Solitude

In the quiet corners of the mind,
Stitches mend what we can't find,
Silence wraps, a gentle bind,
Solitude's peace, a friend so kind.

Each moment, a thoughtful seam,
A tapestry of a lone dream,
In shadows, light will gleam,
In solitude, we find our theme.

Threads of reflection softly show,
In the stillness, room to grow,
With every stitch, we learn to flow,
In solitude, strength we bestow.

A quilt of thoughts, stitched with care,
Each fabric whispers, deep to share,
In the silence, no need to beware,
Stitches of solitude, lightly bare.

So let us cherish the quiet hours,
In our hearts, we nurture flowers,
With stitches of solitude, our powers,
Crafted in calm, where love empowers.

Patterns of Kinship

In the dance of life, we learn,
Patterns of kinship softly turn,
With every twist, our hearts discern,
Connections forged, for this we yearn.

From roots that stretch through time and space,
We share stories, a warm embrace,
In laughter, memories we trace,
In every smile, love finds its place.

Through trials, our patterns strengthen,
In unity, we find true lengthen,
With hands together, hearts we reckon,
In kinship's bond, there's no end threaten.

With colors rich, our lives align,
Each moment shared a treasured line,
In the fabric of love, we shine,
Together, forever, our design.

So let us celebrate this thread,
In patterns of kinship, we're led,
With love as the light we tread,
In every heart, may joy be spread.

Yarns of Yearning

In twilight's glow, dreams take flight,
Whispers of hope in the cool, still night.
Hearts entwined, our wishes weave,
Tales of longing, we believe.

A tapestry rich with every sigh,
Stitches of moments that pass us by.
Under the stars, a soft embrace,
We find our place in time and space.

Each thread a story, tender and true,
Of journeys taken, both old and new.
With every knot, a bond so strong,
Together we flow, where we belong.

In silence shared, a language profound,
With every heartbeat, our souls are found.
We walk the path where dreams are spun,
In the rhythm of life, we become one.

Yarns of yearning, woven with care,
Crafting a future, rich and rare.
With love as our guide, we'll always strive,
In each other's hearts, forever alive.

Knots of Unity

In the gathering dusk, our voices blend,
In laughter and joy, our spirits mend.
We share our dreams, a vibrant hue,
In the fabric of time, woven anew.

Each knot we tie in friendship's grace,
Binds our stories, a sacred space.
Through trials faced and battles fought,
Our unity's strength cannot be bought.

In the dance of life, we find our beat,
Hands together, we move on our feet.
Every challenge met with hearts aligned,
In the tapestry of love, we've combined.

Threads of courage, stitched with care,
In the warmth of trust, we lay our bare.
Through seasons change and skies of grey,
United we stand, come what may.

With every knot, a promise held,
In the warmth of unity, our fears quelled.
Together we rise, never to fray,
In the strength of our bond, we find our way.

Threads of Time

Moments unravel, like threads in the night,
Weaving our lives under soft moonlight.
Echoes of laughter, shadows of tears,
Threads of our history, binding our years.

In the loom of fate, we twist and turn,
Carving our paths, for wisdom to learn.
Each second a thread, fragile yet strong,
In the tapestry of time, we belong.

Through laughter and pain, each pattern brings,
Stories of joys, and the solace it sings.
With every heartbeat, we stitch and sew,
The fabric of life, a beautiful show.

With golden threads, we craft the future,
Woven with dreams, our hearts as the sutures.
As seasons change, we adapt and thrive,
In the evolution of time, we strive.

As dawn awakens, we rise once more,
Threads of tomorrow, we long to explore.
In every moment, let love be the rhyme,
In the endless journey, the threads of time.

Frameworks of Friendship

In the heart's embrace, foundations are laid,
Frameworks of friendship, steadfastly made.
With laughter and trust, we build our design,
Each moment cherished, our bonds intertwine.

In corners of comfort, we shelter our dreams,
Through trials and triumphs, we strengthen the beams.
With every support, a pillar is found,
In laughter's echo, our joys rebound.

Crafting our stories, in colors so bright,
Walls of resilience, holding us tight.
Each beam a memory, each nail a cheer,
In the structure of love, we have no fear.

In storms of life, we weather together,
Our frameworks sturdy, through any weather.
With open hearts and smiles that gleam,
In the architecture of friendship, we dream.

As life unfolds, we'll build and renew,
Creating our spaces, vibrant and true.
In the framework of friendship, we'll always stay,
Together we flourish, come what may.

Tapestry of Time

In shadows of the past, we weave,
Threads of joy and pain, we believe,
Each moment a stitch, in colors bright,
Binding our stories, through day and night.

From laughter and tears, our fabric glows,
In gentle whispers, the history flows,
Patterns emerge, intricate and grand,
A masterpiece forged by life's guiding hand.

Every thread holds a dream, a voice,
In the silence of time, we all rejoice,
Together we stand, in unity strong,
As the tapestry sings its eternal song.

Time marches on, yet we find our way,
In the fabric of life, we choose to stay,
With every weave, a new chance begins,
Creating a world where hope always wins.

So cherish the threads, each unique and true,
For the tapestry's beauty reflects me and you,
As we stitch the moments, both big and small,
In this grand design, we are one and all.

Stitched Narratives

In the heart of a quilt, stories combine,
Soft whispers of old, through lifetimes entwine,
Each patch a memory, a love that we've kept,
In the fabric of dreams, our secrets are slept.

With needles of hope, we carefully thread,
The tales of our past, where adventures led,
In vibrant colors, our histories blend,
Creating a canvas, where journeys ascend.

Fragments of life, cherished and worn,
In stitches of time, new futures are born,
As hands gently guide, the fabric takes shape,
In the art of our lives, we find our escape.

From heartache to joy, we stitch with intent,
In the tapestry's glow, our love is well spent,
For every seam tells the truth of our hearts,
In this quilt of existence, we play our parts.

So gather the scraps, let stories unfold,
With warmth in our hearts, as the memories hold,
A mosaic of lives, beautifully made,
In stitched narratives, our legacies laid.

Echoes in the Loom

In the silence we hear, echoes of yore,
Whispers of souls that came before,
In the loom of time, their spirits dance,
Each thread a journey, a timeless chance.

The rhythm and pulse, of ages gone by,
In the warp and the weft, their stories lie,
With the clatter and hum, memories arise,
A tapestry rich, beneath endless skies.

Every age a color, vivid and bright,
Blending together, both day and night,
In the patterns we find, the truth of our race,
In the echoes of history, we find our place.

Through pain and through joy, the loom keeps its beat,
Revealing the threads that make us complete,
With each woven tale, our legacy grows,
In the fabric of time, the essence still flows.

So listen closely, to the whispers of old,
In the echoes we find, the stories retold,
In the loom of existence, we each play a part,
Weaving the echoes, straight from the heart.

Common Threads

In the dance of creation, we find our bind,
Common threads of life, intricate and kind,
With colors of courage, love, and despair,
Our narratives woven with delicate care.

Through laughter and strife, our patterns unite,
In the fabric we share, there's strength in the light,
Each stitch a reminder, of battles we've won,
In the quilt of our lives, we rise with the sun.

The beauty of differences, stitched side by side,
In harmony's fabric, our hearts take pride,
For every singular thread plays a role,
In the vibrant mosaic that forms the whole.

So together we stand, with hands intertwined,
Embracing the stories that life has designed,
As the tapestry grows, we honor our fate,
In the common threads that forever create.

Let us cherish this weave, diverse yet complete,
In the loom of our lives, where all voices meet,
For the fabric of unity, strong and profound,
Is the tapestry's essence, in love it is found.

Patterns in the Fabric

Threads weave in curious ways,
Colors dance in vibrant hues.
Each twist tells a hidden tale,
In the fabric, life renews.

Beneath the seams, stories lie,
Whispers of time gently spun.
Patterns form, then fade away,
Yet in the weave, we are one.

Through stitches bold, and stitches fine,
Layers build a world defined.
In every knot, a dream untold,
The fabric holds what's intertwined.

Embrace the flaws, the ragged threads,
For imperfection is a gift.
It binds us all, each line we draw,
In unity, our spirits lift.

So let the fabric shape our fate,
In vibrant colors, let love lead.
As patterns shift, we'll find our place,
In the tapestry, we're freed.

Holds Tight in Times of Need

When shadows fall, and hearts grow cold,
A tender hand, a warm embrace.
In moments bleak, we seek the light,
Together we find solace, grace.

The strength we share can move the world,
A bond unbroken, forged in trust.
Through trials faced, we stand as one,
In unity, there's strength robust.

With whispered words, we lift the weight,
A gentle smile to ease the pain.
In silence shared, we find our peace,
In every tear, love's soft refrain.

So when the storm begins to rage,
Hold tight, dear friend, you're not alone.
We'll weather all, let courage grow,
In times of need, our hearts are home.

Together we will face the dawn,
With hope alive, we'll rise anew.
In every challenge, hand in hand,
A bond unbreakable, pure and true.

Grains of Connection

A sprinkle here, a whisper there,
In each encounter, seeds are sown.
Connections bloom in gentle ways,
A web of kindness fully grown.

With every smile, a bridge is built,
Through laughter shared, our spirits blend.
A tapestry spun from the heart,
In small moments, we transcend.

We find our strength in shared stories,
A tapestry woven with care.
In grains of wisdom, we are rich,
Each kernel holds a legacy rare.

As seasons shift and memories fade,
The bonds we forge will hold us tight.
In unity, we'll face the storms,
Together, we'll shine as one light.

So cherish each grain, each fleeting joy,
For in connection, we ascend.
With open hearts, let love unfold,
In every moment, we transcend.

Sewing Seeds of Solidarity

With needle poised and fabric stretched,
We stitch our dreams with hopeful hands.
In every patch, a story blooms,
A quilt of trust that understands.

Together we sow the seeds of change,
In every thread, a vision bright.
As hearts unite and voices blend,
We craft a world where all can thrive.

In solidarity, we find our voice,
Each stitch a promise, strong and clear.
Through shared resolve, we pave the way,
For brighter days that draw us near.

From seeds of doubt to fields of light,
Sowed with care, our dreams align.
A garden rich with every hue,
In unity, our hearts combine.

So let us sew with love and grace,
A tapestry of hope and peace.
In every stitch, we plant our dreams,
Together, may our strength increase.

The Common Fabric

In woven threads we find our place,
Each color tells a story's grace.
The common fabric, strong and true,
We stitch together, me and you.

With every knot, a bond is tied,
Through laughter, tears, we do confide.
In shared moments, joy ignites,
Our hearts unite through days and nights.

Patterns bloom in vibrant hues,
We celebrate the paths we choose.
In every fold, our lives entwine,
A tapestry, both yours and mine.

As seasons change, our threads may fray,
Yet love's embrace will light the way.
Through trials faced, we stand as one,
This common fabric, just begun.

So let us weave with tender hands,
Together crafting shared demands.
For in each stitch, a tale unfolds,
Of unity, of hearts so bold.

Crafting Connections

From distant shores, our voices rise,
With courage found in soft replies.
Crafting connections, heart to heart,
In every glance, a brand new start.

Through whispered dreams, the night ignites,
With hopes that soar like wondrous flights.
Each word we share, a bridge we build,
In kindness, every silence thrilled.

With open arms, we gather near,
In laughter's light, we conquer fear.
With every story freely shared,
The spaces close, the love declared.

In vibrant moments filled with grace,
We find our strength in every place.
Crafting connections that won't sever,
Together, now and forever.

So let us touch the skies above,
And celebrate this gift of love.
In every bond, we find our way,
Creating joy in bright array.

Marrows of Togetherness

In marrow deep, our roots align,
With strength derived from love's design.
Together we stand, a steadfast fleet,
In harmony, our pulse, our beat.

Through trials faced, we learn and grow,
In every challenge, seeds we sow.
With laughter shared, our spirits rise,
Connected hearts, a sweet surprise.

In storms and calm, we face the day,
Holding tight in our own way.
Marrows of togetherness we share,
A bond that flourishes with care.

So let us cherish every thread,
In whispered dreams that lie ahead.
For in this love, we find our song,
A melody that carries long.

Together woven, strong and bright,
Guided by that inner light.
In every laugh, a story flows,
In marrows deep, our friendship grows.

Connections in Every Stitch

In every stitch, a tale is spun,
With threads of gold beneath the sun.
Connections flourish, hearts unveiled,
In fabric formed, no love derailed.

The rhythm steady, beats in time,
As hands unite in perfect rhyme.
Crafting whispers in soft designs,
In every seam, a love that shines.

With needle's grace, we weave the past,
Creating bonds meant to last.
Connections in every stitch we make,
A legacy of love we stake.

Together twined, our spirits soar,
In threads of hope forevermore.
Through shadows deep, we find the light,
In every stitch, our dreams take flight.

So let our hands, with care enclose,
The beauty in the life we chose.
In every thread, a promise feels,
Connections strong, our heart reveals.

Fabricating Bonds

In the quiet dusk, we weave our dreams,
Threads of laughter, silent screams,
With every twist, our stories blend,
In this embrace, we find a friend.

Through trials faced, we stand aligned,
In every heart, a thread confined,
Together strong, we'll share the load,
In the fabric of life, love's road.

With every stitch, our hopes take flight,
In shadows deep, we'll chase the light,
The bond grows tight, no seam to fray,
Hand in hand, we'll find our way.

As colors merge, our spirits glow,
In this creation, we freely show,
The tales we tell, both old and new,
In every strand, my heart with you.

So let the loom of life entwine,
In every moment, your heart is mine,
With every breath, this we proclaim,
Together we are, in love's sweet name.

Colors of Companionship

Beneath the sky so vast and wide,
We paint our joys, our hearts collide,
In hues of laughter, tears of grace,
Together we find our sacred place.

With every brush, our stories blend,
A canvas bright, where hearts transcend,
Each color a moment, bold and true,
In the palette of life, it's me and you.

As autumn leaves in amber fall,
We gather warmth, we stand tall,
In shades of trust, we'll navigate,
Through storms of doubt, we'll celebrate.

When gray clouds loom and shadows creep,
In vibrant bonds, our spirits leap,
With every stroke, we add more light,
Together, we'll make the world bright.

So here's to us, with laughter and cheer,
In this gallery, we hold so dear,
With every hue, our souls entwined,
In colors of love, our hearts aligned.

A Tapestry of Touch

Fingers interlaced, our hearts align,
In whispers soft, your hand in mine,
With gentle strokes, the world unfolds,
In this embrace, our story told.

The warmth of your skin, a sweet embrace,
A tapestry formed in time and space,
With tender threads, our lives connect,
In every heartbeat, love reflects.

Through tangled paths, we'll navigate,
In woven dreams, never too late,
With every touch, our spirits soar,
In soft caress, we find the core.

As seasons change and shadows fall,
With love's strong stitch, we conquer all,
In every clasp, a promise made,
Together we stand, never to fade.

So hold me close, let the world fade,
In this tapestry, our hearts arrayed,
Forever bound, in love's sweet clutch,
We'll weave our lives with every touch.

Embroidery of Emotions

In the fabric of thoughts, we find our threads,
Stitched with secrets, where silence spreads,
With needle and heart, we craft our dreams,
In the art of love, our essence redeems.

Each emotion a color, vivid and bright,
In the depth of darkness, we find the light,
With careful hands, we mend the seams,
In this embroidery, we share our dreams.

Through laughter's joy and sorrow's sting,
We stitch together, the bonds we bring,
With patterns vibrant, our tales entwine,
In this creation, your soul and mine.

As years unfold, the threads may fray,
But in our hearts, love finds its way,
So let us weave through joy and strife,
In this embroidery, we craft our life.

So here we stand, with joy and grace,
In the tapestry of time, our sacred space,
With every stitch, a love profound,
In the art of emotions, forever bound.

Threads of Destiny

In the loom of fate we weave,
Colors bright, in night we cleave.
Each twist and turn, a course unknown,
In quiet whispers, destiny's shown.

Life's tapestry, both soft and bold,
Stories whisper, secrets told.
With every thread, a choice is made,
In shadows deep, our dreams cascade.

Binding moments, stitch by stitch,
In chance encounters, hearts will twitch.
Together we dance, in cosmic flow,
Unraveling paths that shape our glow.

We thread through trials, laughter, tears,
In unity, we face our fears.
A fabric strong, yet fragile too,
Threads of destiny, me and you.

So let us weave a future bright,
With threads of love, we'll chase the light.
Each knot a memory, warm embrace,
In the end, we find our place.

Threads of Understanding

In the fabric of thought, we share,
Stitching feelings with utmost care.
Each gentle word, a needle's grace,
With every story, we find our space.

We open hearts, we dare to see,
The intricate weave of you and me.
Through silent pauses, we connect,
In the patterns, we both reflect.

Each seam a lesson, every tear,
In shared silence, we find what's fair.
Together we mend, together we grow,
Threads of understanding help us show.

In simple moments, harmony sings,
As we navigate the joy love brings.
Through every twist, the warmth we seek,
In threads of understanding, we speak.

Let kindness weave through all we do,
In this tapestry, me and you.
With each connection, a brighter hue,
Threads of understanding, ever true.

Sails of Connection

Across the sea of dreams we sail,
With hearts as anchors, we will not fail.
Every wave a chance to explore,
In the wind of hope, we open more.

Guided by stars, we chart our way,
In the dance of currents, bright as day.
The sails of trust, they fill with ease,
Over horizons, we drift like leaves.

Together we voyage, side by side,
In storms of life, we will abide.
Navigating challenges, hand in hand,
With sails of connection, we make our stand.

Through the tempests and tranquil seas,
We find our strength where hearts agree.
In the journey's embrace, our spirits rise,
The sails of connection reach for the skies.

With laughter as wind, we will glide,
In every wave, our dreams collide.
In the depths of love, we find our course,
Sails of connection, a wondrous force.

The Fabric of Us

Woven tightly, threads intertwine,
In the fabric of us, stories align.
Each moment shared, a strand of gold,
In the warmth of love, we are consoled.

Patterns emerge, both bright and bold,
In the fabric of us, life unfolds.
Through every stitch, our hearts embrace,
In laughter and tears, we find our place.

Crafting memories, rich and deep,
In the fabric of us, dreams we keep.
With fabric soft, yet strong to hold,
Together we weave a tale untold.

Bound by moments, we dance through time,
In the fabric of us, love's perfect rhyme.
As seasons change, and years unwind,
Together we craft the ties that bind.

So let us treasure what we've made,
In the fabric of us, love's parade.
With every thread, a story sung,
In this tapestry, forever young.

Quilted Echoes

In a tapestry of time, we stand,
Voices woven with gentle hands.
Every thread tells a tale untold,
Soft and warm, yet strong and bold.

Memories stitched in colors bright,
Fading echoes of day and night.
Comfort rests on every seam,
A quilted heart, a silent dream.

Fragile moments in a dance,
Finding solace in chance.
Under starry, endless skies,
The quilt of life never lies.

With each patch, our stories blend,
Questions linger, truths we send.
In quiet nights, we find our peace,
As quilted echoes never cease.

So wrap your soul in fabric's grace,
Feel the warmth of each embrace.
Together woven, never apart,
In quilted echoes, we find heart.

Loom of Lives Intertwined

In the loom of lives, we find our place,
Threads of laughter, woven with grace.
Patterns shifting, stories unfold,
Each strand a memory, bright and bold.

Warp and weft, in rhythmic dance,
Every intersection a fleeting chance.
With gentle hands, we pull and weave,
In this tapestry, we learn to believe.

Through shadows long and colors bright,
We craft the fabric of day and night.
Every tug and every thread,
Leaves an echo of love, unsaid.

As lives entwine, the fabric grows,
Bearing the weight of joys and woes.
Together we create the design,
In the loom of lives, our fates align.

So let us gather, hearts entwined,
In the loom of life, we are defined.
Crafting a story, forever twined,
In the essence of love, intertwined.

Patches of Understanding

In patches sewn with care and thought,
Lessons learned, and wisdom sought.
Each piece holds a story rare,
Bridges built with love to share.

Colors blend from light to dark,
Emotions echoed, leaving a mark.
Tender threads of heart and mind,
In patches of understanding, we find.

Stitched together, we stand so strong,
In this quilt, we all belong.
Differences honored, embraced with grace,
In the warmth of connection, we find our place.

The fabric speaks in whispers low,
Binding our souls as we grow.
Through the stitches of our past,
Patches of understanding hold fast.

So let us honor each unique thread,
In this quilt where love is spread.
Together we weave, hearts combined,
In patches of understanding, we're aligned.

Beneath the Surface of Stitches

Beneath the surface of stitches and seams,
Lies a world woven from hopes and dreams.
Threads that shimmer with unspoken words,
A silent bond shared among birds.

With each pull, connections grow,
In hidden layers, love's gentle flow.
Every stitch is a heartbeat's tune,
In a fabric that softly whispers, 'soon'.

Absorbing sunlight, holding the night,
In the depths of fabric, lives take flight.
Woven whispers, alive and real,
Each layer conceals what we feel.

Through shadows cast by fears undone,
Beneath the surface, we are one.
A quilted journey, rich and vast,
In every moment, forever cast.

So touch the fabric with tender hands,
Feel the stories from distant lands.
Beneath the surface, time distills,
In stitches, the heart's truth fulfills.

Fabric of Togetherness

In threads that bind, we find our place,
Woven stories etched in time and space.
Every stitch a tale, every knot a bond,
In this tapestry, we grow, we respond.

Hands reach out in diverse embrace,
Different colors, yet a shared grace.
Each heart a fiber, strong and bright,
Together we shine, a guiding light.

Through storms we weave, with strength we mend,
In unity's dance, we learn to transcend.
Each moment stitched in love's true art,
A fabric of togetherness warms the heart.

As patterns shift, and seasons change,
We find new ways, as dreams rearrange.
In every flaw, beauty breaks through,
In this fabric, I see me in you.

With every thread, a promise we make,
In this journey together, no step we forsake.
Through laughter and tears, we will unfold,
The fabric of togetherness, rich and bold.

Symmetry in Diversity

In the dance of life, we find our grace,
Different rhythms give each other space.
Harmony blossoms in varied tones,
Symmetry shines when individuality owns.

Every voice a note, in chorus we sing,
A mosaic of dreams that each heart can bring.
The beauty of difference in every shade,
Together we flourish, never afraid.

With open hearts, we break the molds,
In the fire of trust, the spirit unfolds.
Like stars that twinkle in the night sky,
Each unique spark, lighting the why.

Embracing the facets that life does impart,
In the art of connection, we play our part.
We celebrate contrasts, the light and the dark,
Symmetry lives where diversity sparks.

United in strength, we boldly ascend,
In the tapestry woven, we find common friends.
Together we thrive, in balance we grow,
In symmetry's grace, our spirits aglow.

Colors of Coexistence

In the palette of life, hues intertwine,
Brushed by the hands of fate's design.
Each color a story, vibrant and true,
In the canvas of coexistence, me and you.

Together we splash in the bright sunlight,
Every shade a whisper, soft and polite.
Distinct yet united, we draw the line,
In this grand masterpiece, your hand in mine.

Through each stroke we learn, our hearts align,
With open minds, our spirits combine.
The beauty of differences paints the scene,
In colors of coexistence, serene and keen.

With every encounter, a new hue appears,
Bringing laughter, joy, even some tears.
No journey is dull when we paint with glee,
In this vibrant world, you're a part of me.

As seasons roll on, let colors blend bright,
Creating a world bathed in love and light.
In the art of coexistence, we stand hand in hand,
Together, we flourish, as one, we shall stand.

An Endless Weave

Threads of connection run far and wide,
In the fabric of life, we all coincide.
With every encounter, a pattern we spin,
An endless weave, where journeys begin.

Together we traverse this winding road,
Each story a thread in this rich abode.
With laughter and love, we stitch and we sew,
Creating a journey wherever we go.

In the loom of the universe, we intertwine,
With hope in our hearts, our dreams align.
Through shared moments, our spirits unite,
An endless weave, glowing ever so bright.

Each loop a memory, held close and dear,
In the tapestry woven, we conquer our fear.
As we navigate life, with courage we strive,
In this endless weave, our souls come alive.

Together we craft a tapestry grand,
Each thread a testament to warmth and to stand.
In the fabric of time, let's cherish the tie,
An endless weave, beneath the vast sky.

Milton Keynes UK
Ingram Content Group UK Ltd.
UKHW022049111124
451035UK00014B/1029